JOHN HIATT
SONGBOOK

Management: Will Botwin, Side One Management

Music Engraving by W.R. Music
Production Manager: Daniel Rosenbaum
Art Direction: Alisa Hill
Administration: Marianne Monroe
Director of Music: Mark Phillips

Photography by Anton Corbijn

ISBN: 0-89524-479-9

Copyright © 1990 Cherry Lane Music Company, Inc.
International Copyright Secured   All Rights Reserved

Edited by Milton Okun

CONTENTS

4
Thing Called Love

8
Have a Little Faith

12
Lovers Will

16
She Loves the Jerk

20
Riding with the King

24
The Usual

26
Slow Turning

30
Confidence Man

34
Lipstick Sunset

38
Paper Thin

43
Thank You Girl

46
She Don't Love Nobody

50
Girl on a String

53
Angel Eyes

56
I'm a Real Man

59
The Way We Make a Broken Heart

62
Heavy Tears

FOLD-OUT FOLLOWS PAGE 32

THING CALLED LOVE

Additional Lyrics

2. And you ain't some icon carved out of soap,
   Sent down here to clean up my reputation.
   And baby, I ain't your Prince Charming.
   Now we can live in fear, or set out of hope,
   For some kind of peaceful situation.
   Baby, I don't know why the cry of love is so alarming. *(To Chorus)*

Ad lib lyrics for fade
Just a crazy little thing called love;
It's just a crazy little thing called love.

HAVE A LITTLE FAITH

Words and Music by
John Hiatt

Additional Lyrics

2. When your secret heart
   Cannot speak so easily,
   Come here, darlin', from a whisper start
   To have a little faith in me.
   And when your back's against the wall,
   Just turn around and you will see
   I will catch your fall, baby;
   Just have a little faith in me. *(To Chorus)*

LOVERS WILL

12

Additional Lyrics

2. Who'll hurt each other all the time
   And never give it a thought?
   Who'll lie about where they've been
   And hope they never get caught?
   Who'll say each other's kisses
   No longer thrill?
   Lovers will. (Lovers will.) *(To Bridge)*

3. Who'll never know what they've got
   Until it's just about gone?
   And whose arms will gather up what's left
   To carry on?
   And who'll stalk that little bit of love
   That hasn't been killed?
   Lovers will. (Lovers will.)

RIDING WITH THE KING

**Words and Music by
John Hiatt**

Moderately, with a heavy beat

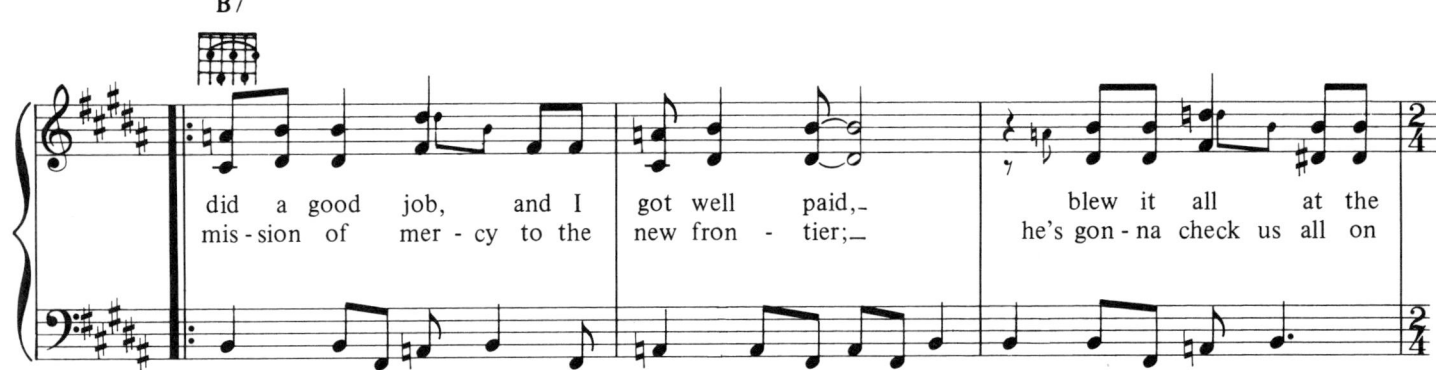

Copyright © 1983 Lillybilly Music (BMI)
Administered by Bug Music
This Arrangement © 1990 by Lillybilly Music
International Copyright Secured All Rights Reserved

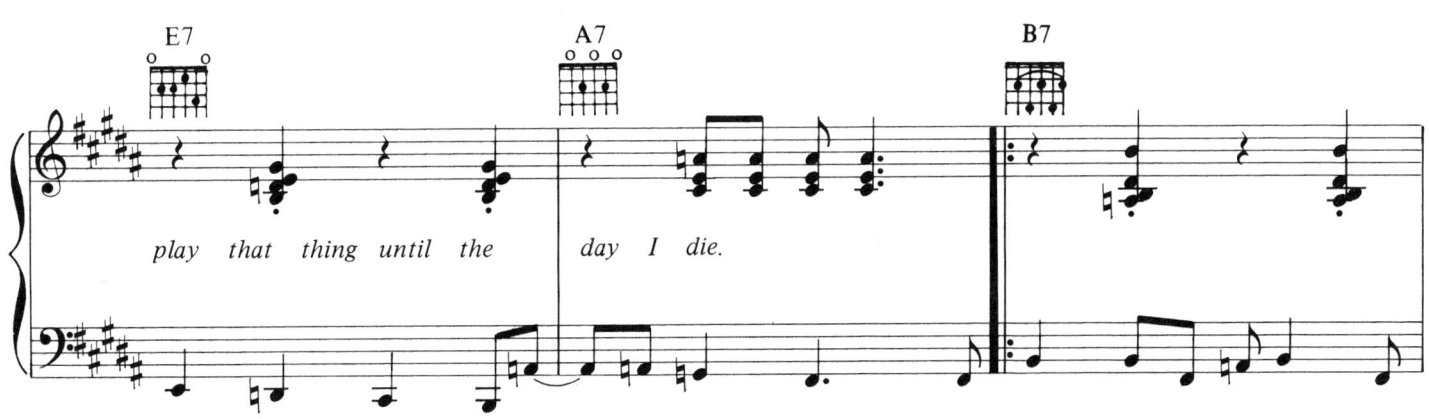
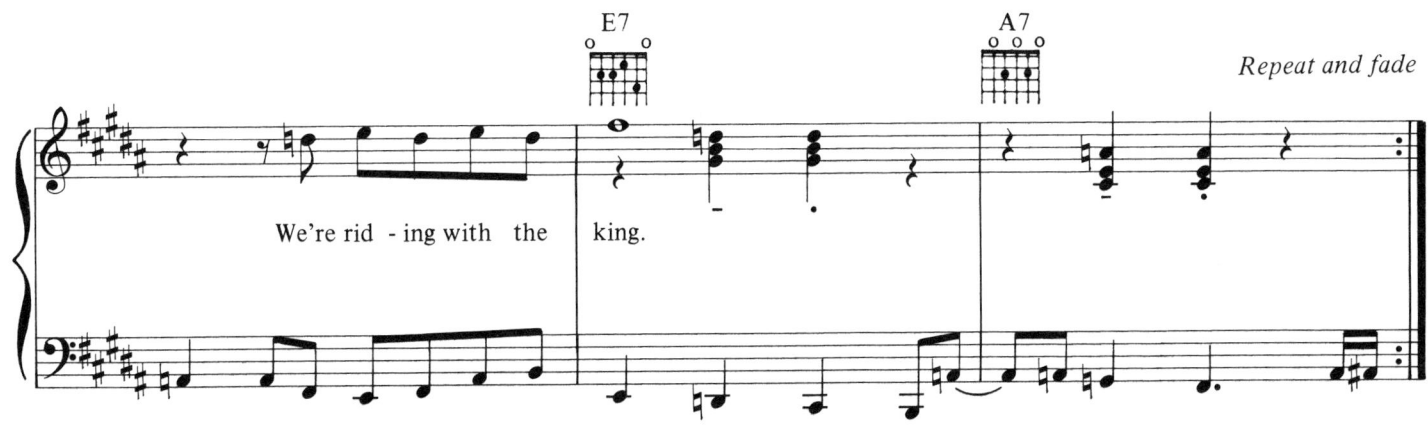

THE USUAL

Additional Lyrics

2. Fifty silhouettes tumbling on the dance floor,
Pink elephants falling through a trap door.
Sixty cigarettes a day, 'cause I'm nervous;
When will that bitch serve us?
I used to be a good boy, livin' the good life,
But fifty thousand kids later, she was a housewife.
She was good, I was unkind;
I'm not thirsty, but I'm standin' in line.

I'll have the usual.
I'll have the usual.

3. Big Jim says the Second Comin's comin';
I think he's just seein' double or somethin'.
You can hang around waitin' for the also-rans;
I can't win, but I seen enough, man.
A fifth of whiskey keeps the doctor away;
A little more and it's Judgment Day.
I had a future, but she just passed out;
I'm gonna drink till I sink, what it is I'm always thinkin' about.

I'll have the usual.
I'll have the usual.

SLOW TURNING

Words and Music by
John Hiatt

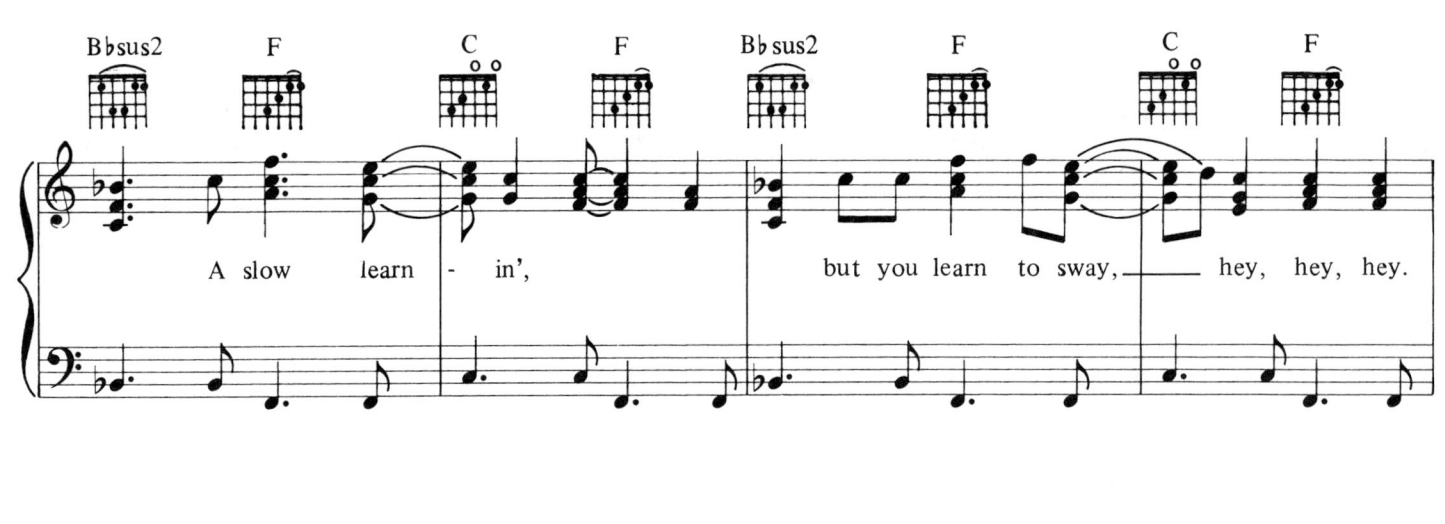
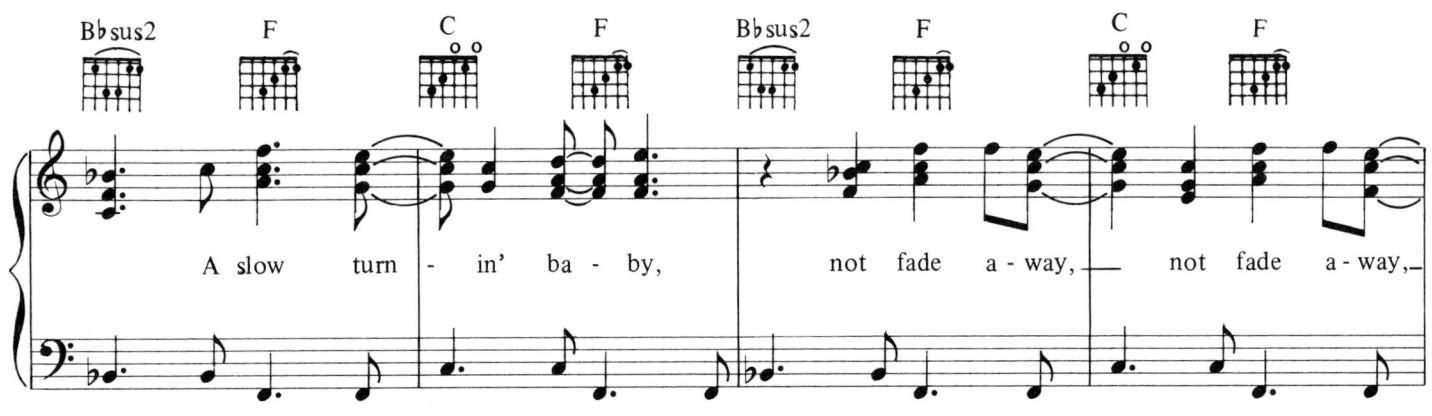
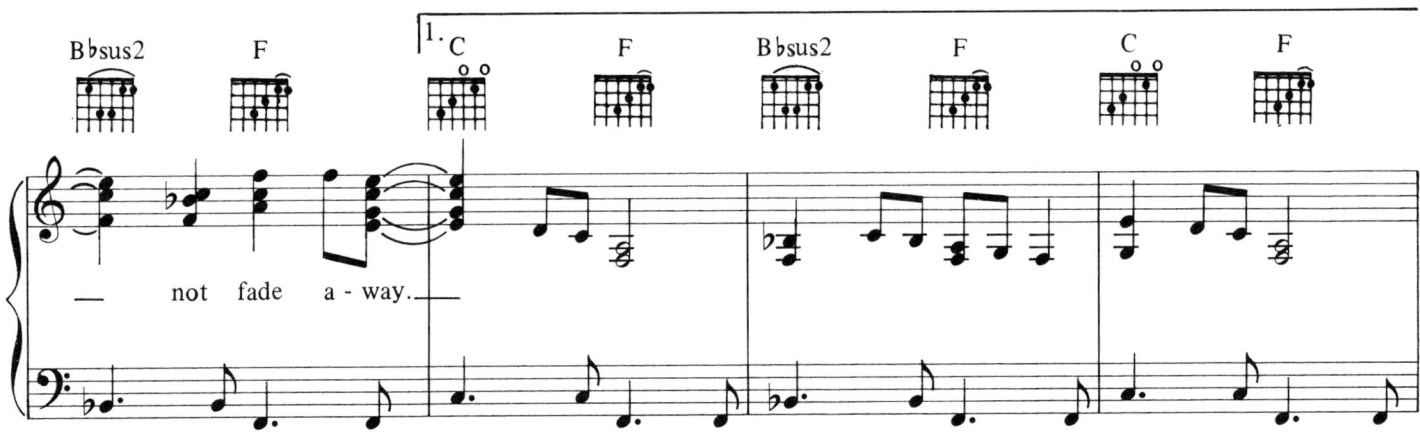
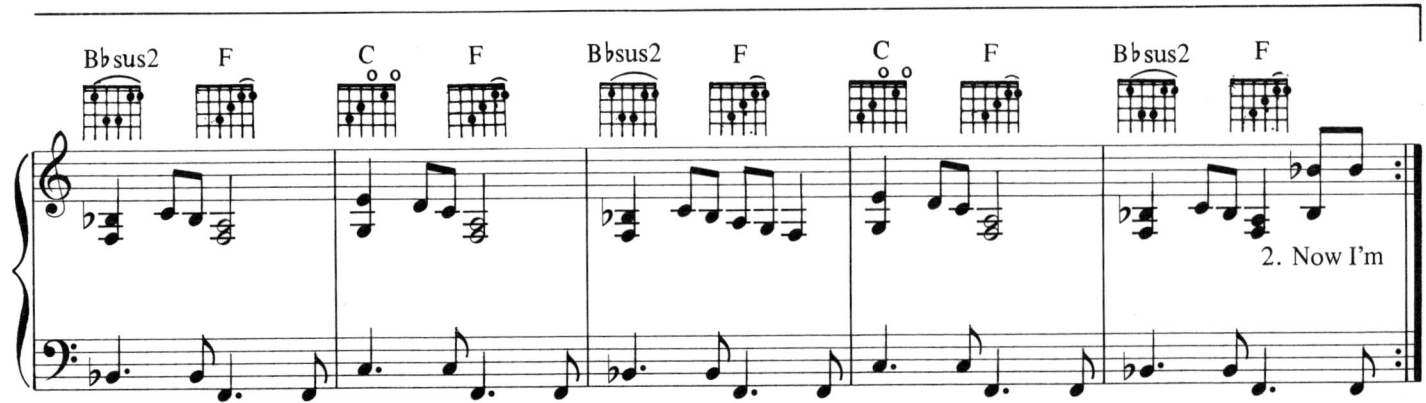

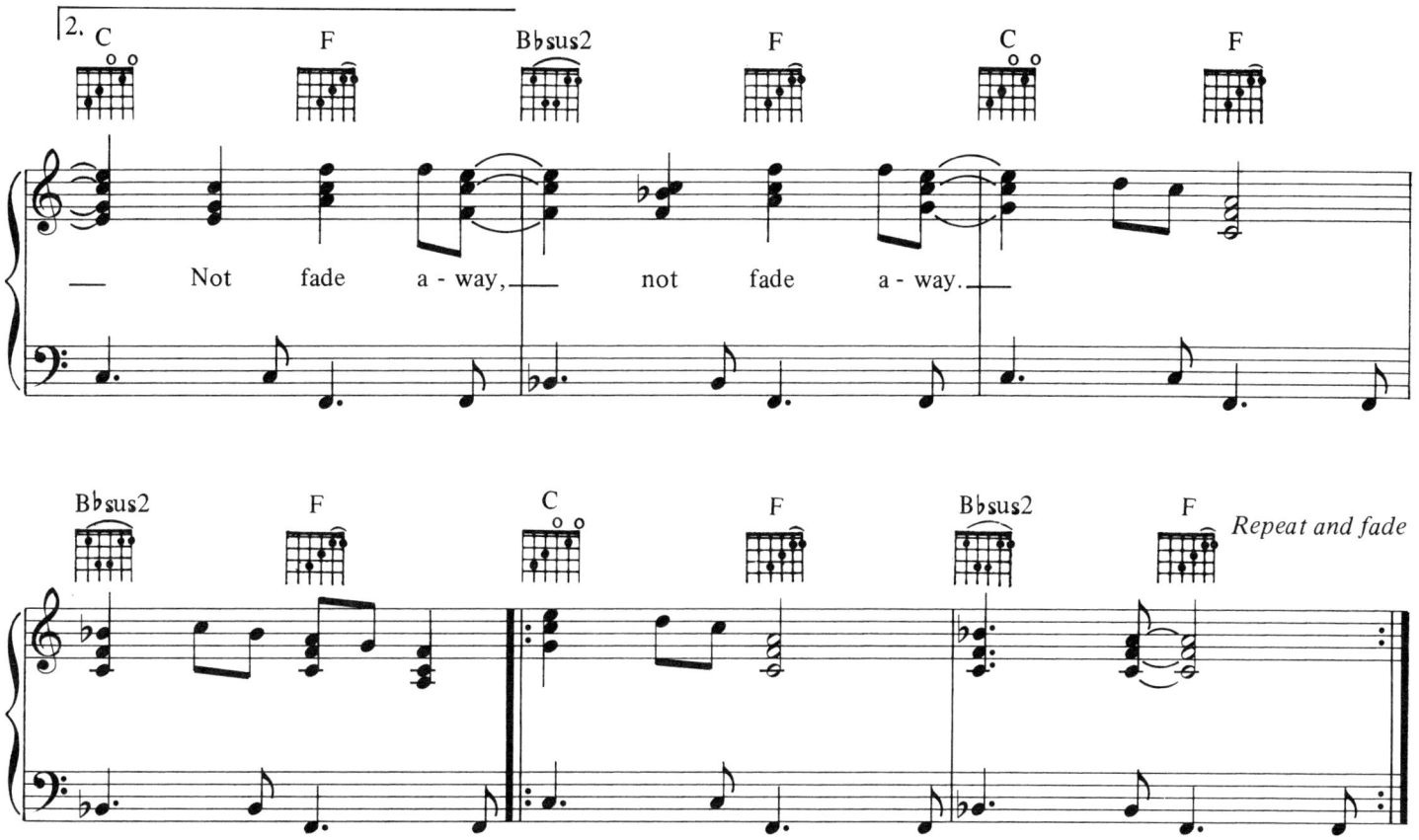

Additional Lyrics

2. Now I'm in my car,
   Ooh, I got the radio down.
   Now I'm yellin' at the kids in the back seat
   'Cause they're bangin' like Charlie Watts.
   You think you've come so far
   In this one-horse town.
   Then she's laughin' that crazy laugh
   'Cause you haven't left the parking lot.
   Time is short, and here's the damn thing about it:
   You're gonna die, gonna die for sure.
   And you can learn to live with love or without it,
   But there ain't no cure.
   There's just a slow turning *(To Chorus)*

Additional Lyrics

2. I can talk old ladies out of all of their money,
   I can talk young girls into callin' me honey.
   You can talk all you want, babe, but I got fast hands.
   You're a real soft touch, but I'm a confidence man. *(To Chorus)*

3. Now, now, now, we were stretched out on the floor, baby, it's all elastic,
   But you stretched it too tight and it snapped like plastic
   And the pieces went flyin' across the badlands.
   No discouraging word could be heard 'cause I'm a confidence man.

4. Now, maybe Chicago is where you're bound,
   But love is a cheaper perfume, it hangs around
   And you roll the dice, now let the bet stand.
   But you can't pull the wool over me, 'cause I'm a confidence man. *(To Chorus)*

LIPSTICK SUNSET

Additional Lyrics

2. Well, a radio was playing,
   And that ol' summer heat was on the rise.
   I just had to get away
   Before some sad old song
   Brought more tears to my eyes.
   And Lord, I couldn't tell her
   That her love was only killing me.
   By the dawning of the day,
   All her sweet dreams would fade
   To a lipstick sunset.

3. Well, it's pretty as a picture, baby.
   Red and blushing just before the night.
   Maybe love's like that for me.
   Maybe I can only see
   As you take away the light.
   So hold me in the darkness;
   We can dream about the cool twilight,
   Till the dawning of the day,
   When I can make my getaway
   To a lipstick sunset.
   There will come another day, *etc.*

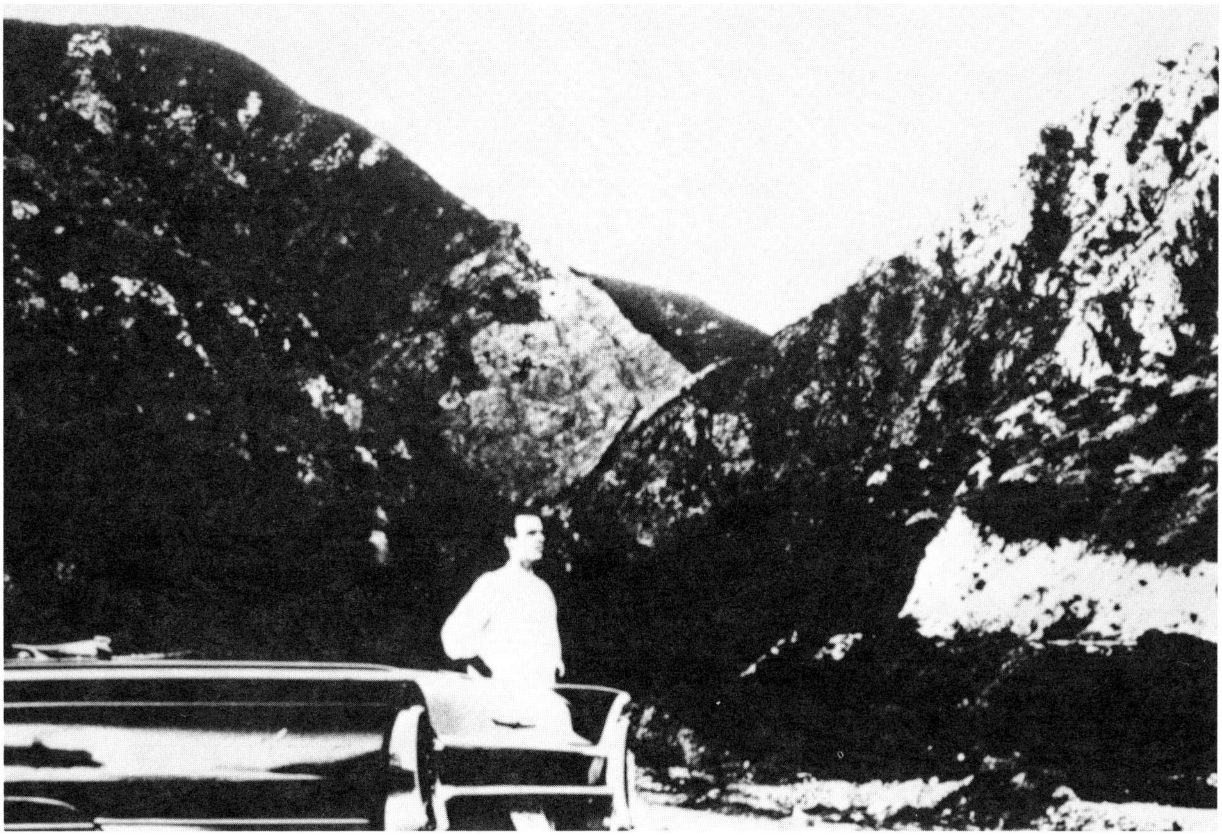

PAPER THIN

Words and Music by
John Hiatt

1. I was gon-na get up off of that bar stool just as soon as I could fig-ure it out.
2. *See additional lyrics.*

Copyright © 1988 Lillybilly Music (BMI)
Administered by Bug Music
This Arrangement © 1989 by Lillybilly Music
International Copyright Secured All Rights Reserved

Why I was o-ver-looked_ at the car_ pool.

Stood up at the dance_ with no_ twist and_ shout.

You're burn-in' with your

last desire, — and ev-'ry mem-'ry haunts you. You write it down in al-co-hol fi - re — 'cause that's the on-ly flame that wants you when you're pa-per thin. — Go on, read all a-bout it. — When you were out of luck, well, luck was

Asus4
Bm
A
Bm
do - in' all right. Now you're pa - per thin. Yeah, they can
E
D
E
D
To Coda
see right through ya. You just cut your lit - tle fin - ger on the
1. F♯
B7
edge of the nigh - yi - yi - yi - yi - yight.
2.
F♯
D.S. al Coda
2. Now do I edge of the night. When you're pa -

edge of the nigh - yi - yight.

You're pa-per thin.

Repeat and fade

Additional Lyrics

2. Now do I really have to be responsible
   For what I did between those tavern walls?
   I was just mixing up some chemicals.
   You could've heard a pin drop, you could've heard time crawl.
   And every once in a while
   You could hear your own heart pound.
   Maybe some paperdoll with a pasted-on smile
   Would let you write her number down. But you were. ... *(To Chorus)*

THANK YOU GIRL

Words and Music by
John Hiatt

rolling in clover, babe; we didn't read this in no tea leaves.
can't help but feeling I'm one up on my brother when night falls.

My fate was sealed before I met you, darling;
'Cause in your arms I get the real love story,

I was halfway down a shallow grave.
no fairy tale from somewhere back in time.

So little room for you to catch me falling; still you took the little love I saved.
In the dawn you're like a morning glory, opening up for my sweet light to shine.

A
I wan-na
thank you, girl;
I wan-na
D
A
thank you, girl.
I wan-na
thank you, girl;
D
1.
A
I wan-na
thank you, girl.
D
E
Esus4
2.
D.S. and fade
It's a
I wan-na

SHE DON'T LOVE NOBODY

Words and Music by
John Hiatt

From my humble point of view, she don't love nobody.
If I could I'd make her mine, but she don't love nobody.
And nothin' borrowed, nothin' blue, she don't love nobody.
And she would never walk that line, she don't love nobody.
Behind the green eyes I
Well, I would give her an-

Copyright © 1984 Lillybilly Publishing (BMI)
Administered by Bug Music
This Arrangement © 1990 by Lillybilly Publishing/Bug Music
International Copyright Secured   All Rights Reserved

D G Em D G
de - tect she don't love no - bod - y. Her
y - thing, she don't love no - bod - y. Well,
C D G Em
heart no kiss could res - ur - rect. She don't love no - bod -
I don't think she's suf - fer - ing. She don't love no - bod -
D G C G D
y. All her life she's been told to hold on tight.
y. All my life I was told to hold on tight.
C G B Em7
There's a man who'd make her his wife, but she's not
There's a girl who'd be my wife, but I'm not

A D C G/B D/A
in - t'rest - ed in an - y - thing ma - ma said.
in - t'rest - ed in an - y - thing ma - ma said. I
G C D G Em
She throws pas - sion to the wind, she don't love no - bod-
want the girl who does not need, but she don't love no - bod-
D G C D G
y. She don't give out what she don't give in.
y. She's the one my heart re - ceives.
Em 1. D G 2. D G
She don't love no - bod - y. And y,

Em D G Em
she don't love no - bod - y, woh, she don't love no - bod-
A D7 G C
y.
D G Em D G
Tell - in' you that girl don't love no - bod - y. She don't
G C D G Em D G
love. Tell - in' you that girl don't love no - bod - y. She don't

GIRL ON A STRING

Moderate beat

Words and Music by
John Hiatt

1. Well, he's got her goin' up and down like a yo-yo, and she never feels better than ever just so-so. Like a shrunken head on a rear-view mirror, she rides along in his atmosphere like

2.3.4. *See additional lyrics*

Copyright © 1982 Queen Isabella's Subject (ASCAP)
Administered by Bug Music
This Arrangement © 1990 by Queen Isabella's Subjects
International Copyright Secured All Rights Reserved

fur-ry dice__ or some voo-doo thing.

4th time to Coda II

He's got that girl on a string,__ girl on a string.__

1.
2. Since they (Girl on a

Chorus

string.) Just__ a lit-tle play toy (girl on a string) for__ the lit-tle bad boy. (Girl on a

2nd time to Coda I

D.S. (take 2nd ending) al Coda I

string.) He's drag-gin' her a-round (girl on a string), he's ty-in' her down. 3. Well, she

Additional Lyrics

2. Since they tied the knot he keeps her in stitches.
   When she ain't banged up she's sewin' his britches.
   Like the line between the orange juice cans,
   She's strung out on his childish demands
   To meet him out by the back yard swing.
   He's got that girl on a string, girl on a string. *(To Chorus)*

3. Well, she carries his baby straddled on her hip bone,
   And there's another on the way, just wait till they get home.
   The deeper in the darkness they get,
   The more she sees that silhouette
   Of a girl, a woman, pretty things ...
   Not that girl on a string, girl on a string. *(To Chorus)*

4. *Repeat 1st Verse*

ANGEL EYES

Words and Music by
John Hiatt and Fred Koller

Slow Rock Ballad

1. Girl, you're looking fine tonight, and ev'ry guy has got you
2.,3. *See additional lyrics*

in his sight. What you're do-in' with a clown like me

is sure-ly one of life's little mys-ter-ies. So to-

Copyright © 1988 Lillybilly Music/Lucrative Music
All rights administered by Bug Music (BMI)
This Arrangement © 1990 by Lillybilly Music/Lucrative Music
International Copyright Secured All Rights Reserved

Chorus
C
Em7
F
G
night I'll ask the stars a - bove,
C
Em7
F
G
F
C/E
3
"How did I ev - er win your love?"
What did I do,
E7
Am
G
F
C
1. G
To Coda
3
what did I say to turn your an - gel eyes my way?
C
G/C
3fr.
F/C
C
G/C
3fr.
F/C
2. G
C
eyes my way? Don't an - y - one

Additional Lyrics

2. Well, I'm the guy who never learned to dance.
   Never even got one second glance.
   Across the crowded room was close enough.
   I could look but I could never touch. *(To Chorus)*

3. There's just one more thing I need to know:
   If this is love, why does it scare me so?
   It must be something only you can see,
   'Cause, girl, I feel it when you look at me. *(To Chorus)*

I'M A REAL MAN

Words and Music by
John Hiatt

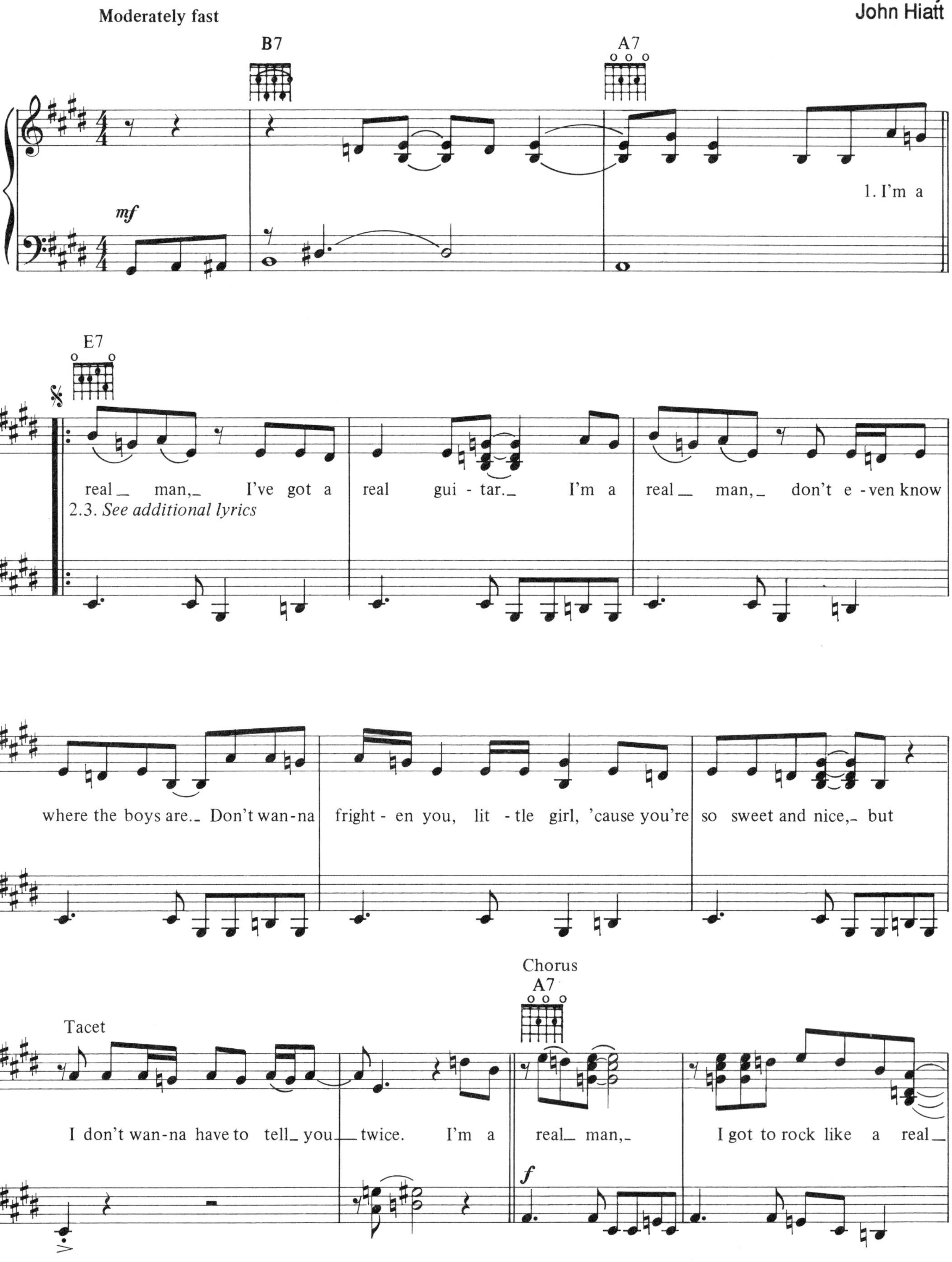

man. Don't get no shock from that el-e-va-tor mu-sic in your com-pu-ter pro-gram. Ba-by, how'd you like to rock with a real man? 2. Yes, I'm a man? Ev-'ry dol-lar I earn, girl, I let it all burn. And if I wind up in jail, *(Ad lib:)* there's anyone of *two thousand, six hundred seventy-two* *women that I know who would* glad-ly go my bail. 3. Now

Additional Lyrics

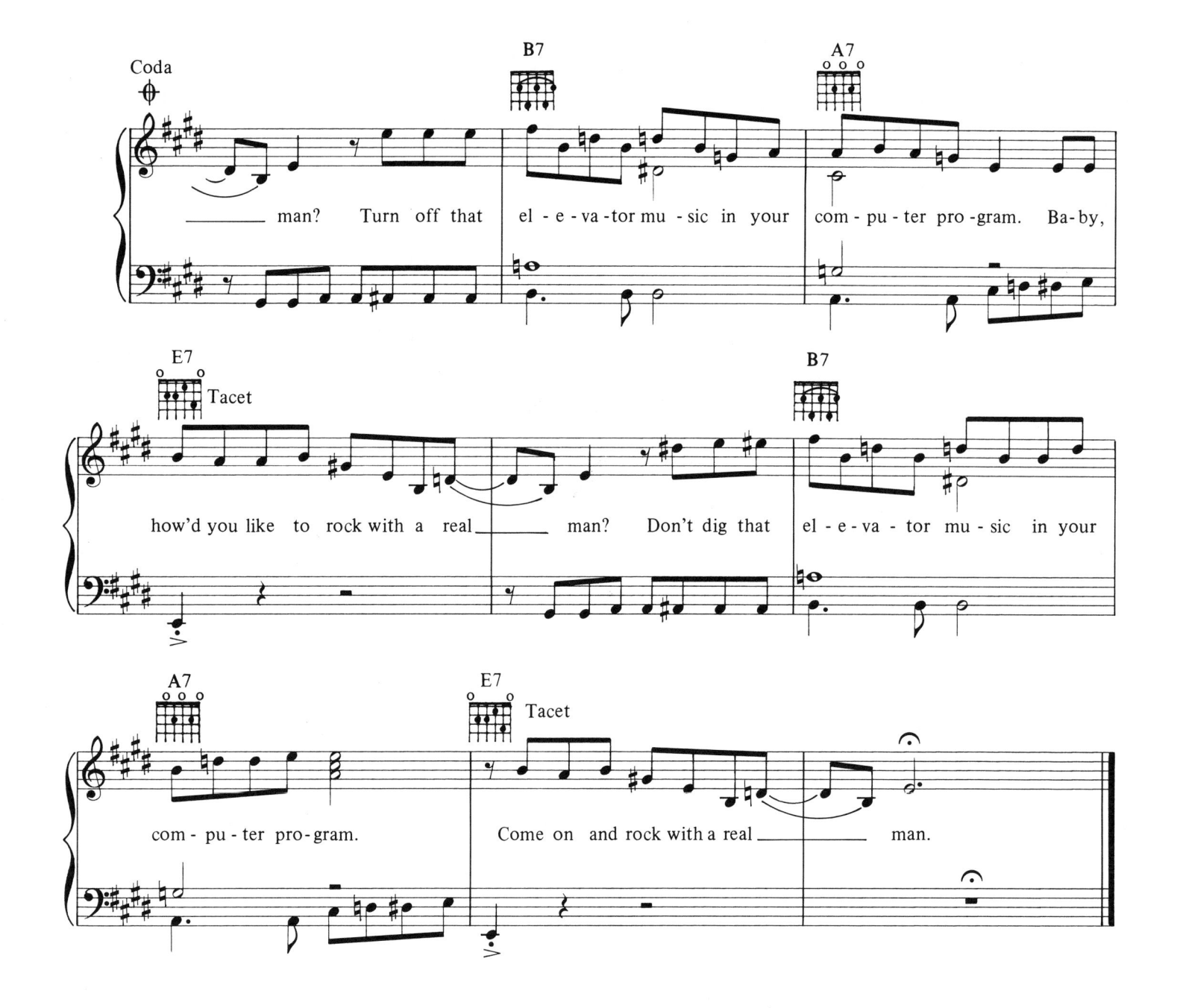

*2. Yes, I'm a real man, baby, I'm not lyin';
   I'm thirty-one years old now, and I still don't mind dyin'.
   You can put the voodoo on me, girl, ain't nothing I can't dodge;
   Just check out this Lincoln in my garage.

   Kids these days, I mean these young pups,
   They're about as wild as Pollyanna after she growed up.
   After a hard day at the Casiotone, man, they just don't wanna live;
   They're 'bout as dangerous as a junior executive. *(To Chorus)*

3. Now you might say I'm just some fool on a boast,
   But how else they gonna hear you, girl, from coast to coast?
   This ain't Dan Rather talkin', this ain't the President's son,
   But baby, I'm still gonna have some fun. *(To Chorus)*

* Play 2nd Verse twice.

THE WAY WE MAKE A BROKEN HEART

Words and Music by
John Hiatt

| G7 | C | To Coda ✛ |

lies, _____ feel-in' ___ sor - ry ____ when she cries, now that the
three _____ when she ___ gets down on her knees and begs you to
new _____ and he'll like-ly ___ hurt her too. There must be

| G | | D |

strings are at-tached, she'll catch on _____ we've done our part. _____
stop at the door just be-fore _____ she comes a-part. _____

| B/D# | Em | C | D |

Oh, _____ this is the way ___ we make a bro - ken heart. ___

| G | 1. C | D | 2. |

Les - son   Now we've

___ laid a trail of tears ___ for her to fol-low, ___ and we've thought of ev-'ry line ___ that she might ___ swal-low. ___ And with

D.S. al Coda

Coda

mil-lions just like you and me prac-ticed in ___ the art. Oh, this is the way ___ to make a bro-ken heart. ___ Oh,

Repeat and fade

HEAVY TEARS

Words and Music by
John Hiatt

Moderately

One day you're hap-py, the next day you're blue. You
May-be she loves you, may-be it's a joke. You
Don't call the doc-tor and ask his ad-vice, 'cause

feel like the whole world's com-in' right down on you.
May-be that fire was just a whole lot of smoke.
he's felt the same way his self once or twice.

Ain't noth-in' wrong but then there ain't noth-in' right, it's
Don't feel warm, but then you don't feel cold, you're
There ain't no cure for the tear in your eye. You

Copyright © 1977, 1978 Tree Publishing Co., Inc.
This Arrangement © 1990 by Tree Publishing Co., Inc.
All rights administered by Tree Pub. Co., Inc. a Division of CBS Music Publishing,
8 Music Square West, Nashville, TN 37203
International Copyright Secured All Rights Reserved

A B E A E C♯m
4fr.
just the kind of thing keeps you up all night.
just get-tin' wea-ry and you're just get-tin' old.
just got-ta sit there, you just got-ta cry.
Heav-y tears in your eyes
B A B E A B E C♯m
Lord, don't they hurt you when you cry? Heav-y tears in your eyes,
B A E/G♯ F♯m7add4 E A
To Coda
when they hit the ground, don't they make a ter-ri-ble sound?
1. 2.
B E A B E B E
And your mind

G♯m
4fr.
C♯m
4fr.
B
A
can't take this wor - ry, and your heart feels un - der - fed. May - be you'll
G♯m
4fr.
C♯m
4fr.
A
B
3
wake up to - mor - row, or may - be you'll just stay in bed.
D.S. al Coda
3
Coda
A
E/G♯
F♯m7add4
ground, ooh, when they hit the
A
E/G♯
F♯m7add4
A
E/G♯
F♯m7add4
ground, I say when they hit the ground, don't they make a ter - ri - ble, don't
N.C.
E6
they make a ter - ri - ble, don't they make a ter - ri - ble sound?
rit.